In My Backyard

I SEE AN ANT

By Agatha Gregson

Gareth Stevens PUBLISHING

Please visit our website, www.garethstevens.com. For a free color catalog of all our high-quality books, call toll free 1-800-542-2595 or fax 1-877-542-2596.

Library of Congress Cataloging-in-Publication Data

Names: Gregson, Agatha, author.
Title: I see an ant / Agatha Gregson.
Description: New York : Gareth Stevens Publishing, [2019] | Series: In my backyard | Includes index.
Identifiers: LCCN 2018013469| ISBN 9781538228777 (library bound) | ISBN 9781538231869 (paperback) | ISBN 9781538231876 (6 pack)
Subjects: LCSH: Ants–Juvenile literature.
Classification: LCC QL568.F7 G724 2019 | DDC 595.79/6–dc23
LC record available at https://lccn.loc.gov/2018013469

First Edition

Published in 2019 by
Gareth Stevens Publishing
111 East 14th Street, Suite 349
New York, NY 10003

Editor: Therese Shea
Designer: Sarah Liddell

Photo credits: Cover, pp. 1, 7, 24 (antennae) TeeTee Photo/Shutterstock.com; p. 5 Fhaizal Mazlan/Shutterstock.com; pp. 9, 24 (colony) irisphoto1/Shutterstock.com; p. 11 Torychemistry/Shutterstock.com; p. 13 KlzTH/Shutterstock.com; p. 15 Marian Fil/Shutterstock.com; p. 17 Dr Morley Read/Shutterstock.com; p. 19 Pavel Krasensky/Shutterstock.com; p. 21 Shutter_M/Shutterstock.com; p. 23 Nixx Photography/Shutterstock.com.

Printed in the United States of America

CPSIA compliance information: Batch #CW19GS: For further information contact Gareth Stevens, New York, New York at 1-800-542-2595.

Contents

I see an ant!
It's in my yard.

Its head has
two antennae.
It smells and touches
with them!

Ants live in groups.
An ant group is a colony.

Most ants live in nests.
Some nests are soil
or sand.
Some are wood
or leaves.

Some ants are workers.
They build the nest.

Workers find food.
This ant found a cherry!

Some ants are soldiers.
They guard the nest.

The ant queen lays eggs.

There are many kinds of ants.

I love to watch ants!

Words to Know

antennae

colony

Index